Good Kitty Diaries

A Sequel to *Bad Kitty Diaries*

Siena Norwich

Printed in the United States of America
First Edition, 2025

ISBN: 978-0-578-73235-0

All potentially identifying details therein that may allude to locations or individuals have been altered to protect the privacy of the author and other possibly perceived individuals. Any similarity to personages living or dead is coincidental and should not be inferred.

Good Kitty Diaries

A Sequel to *Bad Kitty Diaries*

Siena Norwich

"Take courage, my children, and cry to God,
for you will be remembered by him who brought this upon you.
For just as you planned to go astray from God,
return with tenfold zeal to seek him."

Baruch 4:27-29[1]

---

[1] *The Holy Bible: Revised Standard Version*. San Francisco, California: Thomas Nelson Publishing for Ignatius Press, 2006.

Caput Unum

I.

At 15,000 feet you stop talking. You joked on the ground. Admired jet streams. Watched FAA men in collared shirts sweating under the hanger. “Men lose their lives,” I was told, "when they overestimate themselves.”

They pick a smaller and smaller parachute because they want to go faster, but at 120 mph in the air, their bodies don't expect how light they now are. They fall at unexpected speeds. Their watches flip digits too fast and chutes deploy too late.

I came here alone. On the ground, a man named Jack took his shirt off. Overwhelmed by his confident grace as his cotton shirt slipped over his nose, my eyes were glued to the green military strategy book in my lap. A book X gave me weeks before to teach me how to navigate the workplace. Not seen here often: a young woman alone. Jack gave me a gentle smile he repeated later in the plane. Only woman in the cabin, goggles pinching my cheeks. Tenderness to the new convert.

These men bear the gift of reassurance better than most parents. Hourly, they strap strangers like infants against their abdomens and plummet from heaven. Cold. Mouths bullied by wind that beat their bodies that feel so small, shrinking like bugs from the plane. Spiders from the nest.

They inch towards the door. God of parachute. God of helmet. God of wristwatch. Trinket names for fate. State of the art equipment, they repeat while sunning themselves on a picnic table, drinking water.

These men live in a world unknown by most. Ground bound angels obsessed with technique and timing.

“Most people don’t realize you don’t want to die as much as they do,” Jack said, the proclaimed record breaker. When he broke his record for the highest skydive in the state, at that time, they needed oxygen tanks in the plane to get that high up.

Jack was an instructor scolded weeks before for smacking students. The smiler. In the plane, he said, the students zone out and don't hear you. It sets in where they are, this cramped cold can over clouds. Jack would shout, "Wake up!" and smack them upside the head. Just like the army.

Tumbling lifted gate clatters like steel vertebrae. Wind roars into the cabin only minutes before was a ghost thrumming walls. Hooks dig into armpits.

"We're all thinking the same thing. You'd be crazy not to. But you focus on something else. Fear will kill you before the ground."

They rehearse it under the hanger. Cross your arms. Make your body a banana. Head back. Legs together. Wait for my tap. They have you watch a video and replicate your initials a dozen times on a waiver. A man with a long red beard and denim shirt greets you in the introductory video, fingers knit atop mahogany desk, as he recites, "We are not responsible for gross negligence or equipment malfunction because there is no perfect pilot, no perfect parachute, and you are exchanging your life for the thrill of a lifetime."

At your third thrill, you tuck your purse in the corner and you're fifty pounds lighter than last time. You'll fall faster. The first time felt the slowest, like all orders of initiation.

The men ask why you lost the weight, and you blame work while smoking. Ultimate experts of calm.

II.

Skydiving reminds me of BDSM. At cursory glance both appear outlandish excursions from our narrow circles of existence.

If done correctly both entail a clear consent signal system requiring two parties to negotiate power. If you don't want to jump, communicate this to your instructor. If you've reached your limit, sound the safe word.

An obsession with minutia. Wear a parachute of darker color to see when the sun fades it and material is thinning. Soak your braided jute rope in cold water to tighten fibers. Breathe through your nose.

At 15,000 feet I still thought of X as the wind baptized my scalp and I didn't know which way was up. Like being tumbled by a cold wave. X was in my heart as I plunged to the earth. I could climb the altitude with ten men, hook myself to someone and release my life to the winds and still live deep in the cavity of my longing. X all the way below, tapping a keyboard and sipping coffee, would never know even miles apart in the stratosphere, his name was printed on my tongue, raised purple like a scar.

III.

"Just act like a human instead of a robot," my employee told me. Mid-meeting in a large room on the third floor. We had to have this meeting in a space this size because I was told my employees were focusing on their "psychological safety" after I informed them of a missed deadline. "Psychological safety" was a term they learned at a human resources seminar I requested they attend for their annual performance review.

An idyllic locale of collegial equity defined

as: an employee's freedom to voice procedural distress, imaginative inquiry, and an overall feeling of validation without scalding rebuke. We were in this room to cultivate a "brave space" because "safe space" wasn't enough anymore. My employee missed a deadline, agreed to in writing months prior, and exacted a language of personal implication against me.

The fidgety bird-like way he placed his pen adjacent to his notepad, looking down in solemn reflection, he stammered, "You always have this take-charge attitude like my feelings don't matter. Sometimes I-I feel like the Robin to your Batman."

Everyone laughed except me. Never lifting my eyes, pen slurring cursive. I thanked him for expressing his viewpoint: this is what the workshops suggest managers do upon feedback.

IV.

At the gun range an interstate away, skirting speed limits mid-morning, I stood enchanted as hot shells flew into my booth, glancing my wrists like bee stings.

"Are you sure this is your first time?" my instructor asked, lip ring catching the fluorescent bulbs above. The cowboy in the booth next us dispelled shells the size of my baby bird thumbs that leapt toward my blouse.

I gasped the first time my instructor said, "Breathe and pull it slowly."

My body jerked back like an orgasm, fingers cold under warm barrel, ears aching from muffs. My instructor continued, woman to woman, "Never let a man micro sell you, they see a girl like you and think they can pull one off."

V.

I gave X my best target. I was smelling it all night, 9mm burnt paper holes. Sig Sauer P320. In the past, on occasion, X taught me a stance in the back office.

Teacup with your hand. Knees shoulder width apart. Dominant eye level with your thumb. As he stood next to me, I became increasingly aware of how tall he was, dwarfed and dumb as the corner of my eye registered the slow rise of his chest with every breath, heathered gray cotton cresting near my shoulder. Staring ahead, ears burning. Breathe and pull it slowly.

VI.

I don't like to visit the neighborhood. The shock of green never fades. Living years of hot asphalt, warm piss breath subway and sneakers wet from sunrise street cleaners, make me feel dirty in the suburbs. Manicured flower beds. Kitschy mailboxes with toy motorcycles. Lawns. Shrubs. I'm a mutated germ that will annihilate itself in these suburbs.

As I grow older and revisit this place, I realize the ghost of desire in that wan gaze of the gas station cashier was far too real. Not contrived from too many movies. Not embroidered by too many novels. These lonesome suburbs are inflamed by a dusty window fan.

I pretend not to notice the cashier's prolonged animal eye contact while counting change on the counter. Through his limp greasy bangs bunched by a hair net and bulging mantis eyes, this cashier was and will: find a girl like me somewhere someday, if he is not already bound by her curse and reviving her memory in another.

By every unlit midnight strip mall and stalled parking lot engine, he will snicker back, "Are you sure you only want one pack of cigarettes?"

A tornado destroyed half my hometown. I was told growing up tornadoes couldn't come here, too many hills. This dispelled childhood fantasies of whirlwind debris and vicious hail stones. Then the local horticultural school completed a ten-year experiment: the cultivation of the Corpse Flower. *Titan Arum*, three meters high. It took years to grow and when it bloomed it smelled like dead bodies.

News reporters came from all over. A brief glimmering media splash in an otherwise overlooked school. A plant whose primary talent an assault on the senses. Pride of my hometown.

A buzz of intrigue revisited the area. Their olfactory oddity and unconventional wisdom for beauty renewed interest state-wide in a quiet pocket of the county. Like a cracked heirloom doll, this death plant waited smug with supplicants at its feet. Gardeners who'd tended this plant daily, smacking dirt out of their gloves on their knee and squinting away from the cameras, described their effort to tend this entity into existence, like doomed midwives, to the Corpse Flower.

Two months after it bloomed, a tornado came through. It was supposed to be a severe thunderstorm. Winds picked up. Alerts shrieked during *Wheel of Fortune.* My half-blind mother hobbled to the basement with handfuls of jewelry. My father stood on the steps consenting to be blown away.

It ripped off roofs. Destroyed houses. Demolished the horticultural school. Trees resembled burnt match heads. Trees that took centuries to reach their towering beauty ripped bare like raped virgins. Branches splintered across hoods of cars. Acres ragged with debris. Blistered tracts of land. The curse of the Corpse Flower: my hometown.

I don't like to visit the house. My parents' house. It has a similar haunting as the Corpse Flower. Once a stunning plot, has become the home of an apathetic elderly couple. A source of resentment from young mothers grinding teeth over strollers and submitting complaints to the township about unshoveled snow sidewalks. The neighbors insist their mice came from this place, with azalea bushes hairy and harangued by weeds obscuring windows.

My parent's house is the witch's house. All around maintained, tarped driveway motorboats and glittering porch pinwheels roused by suburban breeze. My parent's home stands apart like the deranged eldest child. Unkempt hair, long nails. Its secret habits manifest in ivy hugging the chimney, a rusted black rocking chair.

I don't like to visit the house. Animal urine greets you before flipping on the light. Cat turds crunch under your sneakers like marbles. The dishes from the last time you were here, that you cleaned, are still piled on the table. Reams of dog hair circle the carpet in partial hieroglyphics. Cabinets I remember white growing up are now brown. I grab the sponge and absorb myself in scrubbing. Back turned. Running water hides a fraction of syllables spoken to me in the kitchen. I offer engagement every other sentence. But I know why their friends don't come here anymore. My mother's eyesight is failing and she cannot walk. She is spared the room I am desperately cleaning.

VII.

The words have left you. They only come with the widest water of loneliness to traverse when words are your only companion.

Your chest cracks when you stretch. Your body does not ask for what it knows it will be denied.

I've privately termed it the 'wave of unreality'. A sudden fear of ungrounded bodylessness. My shrinking body, my conquering of space, burbles into my brain and makes me dizzy. Marveling at the cartography, I chart new signs: thin wrist (lighthouse eddying from arm), knobby knee (rocky outcropping veiled by skirt), slim starling neck (faceted granite obelisk).

When X sits beside me talking at length of the Assyrians or the Phoenicians and I start to feel empty and ill, the 'wave of unreality' approaches. I comb my fingers back from my hairline to ground myself. I keep my discomfort at undetectable levels as I become increasingly aware of my breathing- how little I'm swallowing- how tight my clothes feel. All appears sudden and foreign as fabric congeals to my epidermis in grating unseen embrace. I'm not inhaling. This movement towards reduction is working inward. As the wave of unreality consumes me, my lack of eye contact encourages X to talk more. He is compelled by my detachment, a challenge to warrant more interest. I am a shiny teapot for him to admire himself in.

Hours are easy without food. Cover it with small talk. Iced coffee melts to resemble creek water, interspersed by nicotine bouts. At night, your fingers are sticky from preparing a meal you won't eat.

“Someone's hungry,” he said hours earlier, as you described a dinner, you’ll make but won't eat. Buttery garlic salmon, slick savory squash ravioli and creamy peppered cauliflower.

Soul at the expense of the body, I’ve chosen to renounce where sin first came. Mouth sealed. Eyes hollow.

Living alone in a world evident of private equations. Silent obedience to a polished isolation. Like a shiny teapot. I review the past, pictures enter me like phosphene germs, affections reversed by the minute.

Capitulum Secundum

I.

She was a twin but the twin died. Forever searching for her other half.

Once she was stationed in a hospital for lepers and nursed a woman with breast cancer. One evening she collected the necrotic fluids from the breast sores of this woman into a bowl and drank it. To reach a greater understanding of human pain, the willful ingestion of agony. Made perfect through suffering.

Once she had a vision of marrying Jesus. Fluttering from his cumulus bower to proffer a wedding ring made from his foreskin. This was her vision according to her confessor, Raymond of Capua, circa 1368.

It's said when they smuggled Catherine of Siena's decapitated head out of the country they were stopped by guards. They demanded the bag that contained her lovely visage. When seized, it revealed not her rotting head, blanched and bloated like a foul mushroom, but a bouquet of roses.

Miss Siena, whose family rejected her, living alone in a sequestered corner of the house, taking her shrinking meals, head bent in prayer that would transmogrify radiant and rebellious as roses at a border check. Crossing countries, her scalp softened by spittle from laughter.

I wear her face in secret. Under my blouse. Melancholy Jew longing for the saint centuries away. The woman who let her body destroy itself with a fortress of fantasies implanted in her eye. Skin tightening around bird bones in a body– a poor conduit between eternities at conjecture. Dying– a sweet, strange tapestry stained with tears– pinched between fingers like rosary beads. She starved to death. My spiritual pen pal.

II.

"Meika hates white girls, they had to transfer her last roommate," they told me that morning in the behavioral ward, thirteen years ago, huddled around a T.V. covered by plexiglass.

Meika was short and braided her hair for hours in the bathroom. A plastic mirror foggy with scratches. Meika asked if she could sing to me.

When I exited the shower, she looked at my feet in horror, asking why they were so red. Meika was there for "anger problems" like many other black girls, but not for the same reason as my newfound item of interest, Kaitlyn.

Kaitlyn kept quiet to her notebook nobody was permitted to read. She arrived on a gray December afternoon a month before me in her school uniform. This increased the fervor of our speculation. Green eyes and black hair, she only mentioned an occurrence in the woods with PCP.

Line up. Empty your pockets.

If you don't go to group session, they mark it on their sheet and you're a day farther from discharge. That's all we talked about.

Discharge, discharge, discharge. Never mind what you learned last week, like how to get the blade out of your dad's orange disposable safety razor with a pair of toenail clippers. That flimsy strip of steel whose corner felt like dragging a feather.

"How many of you are here because of a boy?" the new counselor asked in group session.

A room of a dozen minors, some of us turned to each other in shock at this question, others studied their cuticles while cross legged on the carpet. I was appalled. Was it true that all of us here, entrusted into the care of the state, could have signed over our short lives to a grim institution because we could not cope with a cad boyfriend? Was it that simple?

And what if it was true? Our first true taste of love as we knew it, or someone with long blue fingernails raped by a frat boy in a sleeping bag after snorting cocaine, could have been here because of a "boy"?

III.

"How could you let this happen? I have forty people assigned to review this tonight. You mean to tell me they can't even access the work right now? This is really upsetting, this is egregious."

In the office, their voicemails start off calm. Name. Position. Reason for calling. Seconds pass. Anxiety climbs into their voice, a faltered recitation of dates, breathy summary of concern. Shouldered expectations. Articulated timeline. Consequences of subverting said deadline.

"How could you let this happen? The first week?" concluding their phone call with a sobering recollection of themselves. Your voicemail is the faceless receptacle of their pained journey back to a hard-won composure. An angry client. Please. I am this person. Call me at this number. As soon. As. Possible…

Red winking eye of your answering machine registers the demon inside. Enter your passcode to repeat recent messages.

The emails are worse. They are panicking.

None of this was your fault. You did the work of four people in understaffed circumstances. You processed orders and conducted correspondence after hours.

But there was one person: hidden in the dense bureaucratic foliage that failed to do their job. A lapse in labor unnoticed until they let it slip. Typed as they sat sipping chamomile tea in pajamas 'working remote': that they failed to do their job: that suddenly all your work was for naught. One person did not do their job. Anywhere else they would have been fired.

You languish in reveries of revenge. Vivid visceral scenarios. Of said person, who failed to do their job: burning alive in their car, choking against their seatbelt as tears stream down their face and their wet cheeks twinkle from the flames on the hood of their car. Having their legs amputated in phased upward segments, if rescued. Going blind and deaf at once while frying an egg 'working remote': a grease fire consuming their apartment and pets. Their loved ones succumbing to terminal cancer and their final words, clotted by phlegm and groaning aloud to said person: that they hate them as much as you do.

Mid-daydream at your desk, a gentleman approached you. A stranger you somewhat know came by your office. Someone of occasional interaction, asked if you knew the time for mass today at the church a block away. A passing inquiry from an acquaintance, you looked it up.

After he left, you decided to go yourself. Voicemails aggregating, emails staggering, but that lone vow: I will make time to attend mass today. You'd never been to one before. Your fingers tapped keywords, searching. You learned and went.

IV.

I was hardly on time. The front doors locked. Circling the side of the building, looking for an alternate entrance, I found my way in.

"Hello?" I called out. Walking a hall hoping to see a chapel only to find an empty break room. A dusty foosball table. A dark kitchen. Milky light from a small window shining off metal counters. No one. I called out again.

Found the stairs, reached the doors, and opened them with a forceful agony, expecting them to be locked, they swung open. Everyone silent, the priest mid-sentence.

Took a seat in the back. Inventorying surroundings, I observed a bookshelf with which

I assumed prayer books, untouched of dim diluted green. An old lamp with a box underneath.

Many prayers the attendees knew the response for, word for word multiple sentences. I thought of them. Who are these people? Between shifts? Do others know where they are? Or are they secret interlopers like me? Dawdling doe-eyed expecting every door to be locked, unaccounted for by bosses and boyfriends on their lunch break?

Off the radar. Occupying the unnamed untouchable realm of God.

They kneeled, I kneeled. The carpeted floor hurt my knees. Some leaned on chairs in front of them. Heads bent.

I watched the priest and admired the careful symmetry of his posture, eucharist over cup.

I was robbed of the comfort of their rehearsal. A practice they'd inhabited here and elsewhere of total alien experience to me. I watched but did not repeat their words or actions. Hands folded at my stomach, fingers shifting rings on my knuckles, studying the walls.

All lined up in the center before the priest. Some affixed their actions with gestures of personal gentleness: an extra bow, a clasped hand at chest. I observed all like an illiterate child in sheer imitation.

I was last in line before the priest. They bowed and accepted the eucharist. It was my turn. I was hesitant, like a wanderer with cautious steps towards a cliff, asking myself if I saw what I thought I did, that mysterious shapely shadow of love loping between our shoulders. Like a rabid animal among us. The vague unknown beauty of belief.

"Are you Catholic?" the priest whispered in my curls as I looked down at the hem of his vestment.

"No, I'm a Jew, I'm sorry," I said.

He placed his hand on my hair, stiff from gel, and said he would pray for me.

I returned to my seat. Hands clenched at stomach. Tears burning paths down my powdered cheeks, swallowing a sting of rejection. This was the place I turned to in my time of need and not even here could room be made. No soft corner in the soul of God to abide an inch for the Jewess.

A blonde boy with large unblinking eyes approached me after mass and asked my name. I spoke with the priest. He informed me I was denied the eucharist because that is for practicing Catholics that live the faith daily. I could feel the word Jew unspoken between us. We stand, us placeless Jews, fingers hooked in fences, tissue-thin striped pants. Jew.

I thanked him and returned to work.

Capitulum Tertium

I.

"Lie on your stomach," she told me. My cheek against white cotton sheet looking at the wall. Bedside metal rail inches from my nose. I never look while they do these things. I submit to their wand like slick cold marble sliding down my spine.

"Are you comfortable?" she asked.

"I'm alright," I muttered, shifting my face toward the monitor.

Grainy gray: muscles, sinews, tissues reduced to an alien monochrome landscape. A storm stirring, shadows colluding, to create a mass. Sac beneath sand dunes, a wordless world.

My insides a serrated plain, the colorless negative of my entrails.

"You'll know by Friday."

II.

"Do we take the cross too far?" the young priest asked. My eyes watered from incense as I sat near the exit.

"Do we take it too far? The cross was an instrument of death. If you saw someone with an electric chair tattooed on their arm, or had pictures of an electric chair around their house, you would be scared, wouldn't you? What's the difference?"

Everyone's posture stiffened. A father with two young daughters whispered in their hair five pews ahead of me.

"You can scarcely look around this room and not see a cross. Don't even try to count. Why is the cross any different from the electric chair? Or the hangman's noose, or the guillotine? And we worship it. We replicate this image of torture around the very mirror of our cars."

My fingers clenched the melody pamphlet, Latin that may as well have been my

Hebrew. The Jew standing alone, studying surroundings like I had in many bars and clubs. An anxious voyeur as the young priest continued, "His blood soaked that wood and made the cross the tree of life."

III.

"The only person you ever really have is yourself," she told me. Kneecaps buckling like crushed blossoms. Her oily mouth shimmered from the lights above us. The silhouette of her pubic hair as she bent over, small tufts peeking out of satin thong. I slid a twenty in her glitter pink cowboy boot. She laughed and held my hand. I apologized for how cold it was.

"You are all you have in the end," she whispered, her breath warm on my neck as I sunk further in the red vinyl armchair. Her nail slid down my calf, its glossy rounded point grazing my leg. The beefy blonde with crunchy wet curls appeared in the doorway.

"Time's up."

IV.

"We pray for the intentions in the hearts of those present," Father recited, eyes closed and hands at chest.

"We live in very counterculture times," he continued, eyes settling on podium, "But sometimes I think the most counterculture thing we can do is pray because it's a sincere hope for change."

V.

"Can I tell you a secret? I once had a relationship with a guy here. We can get in trouble for that," she went on, I nodded while watching her prawn pink acrylic nails roll a blunt on the bar top.

"I really loved him, but he got me sick and denied it."

I apologized to her. She bobbed her head while speaking but wouldn't look at you, chirpy and smiling. Dimpled chin wagging toward rhinestone bra, hardly looking up. She said she was once in a commercial for a local vegan restaurant.

"I'm stuck here. It's $300 for a permit and nobody hops between places. It's too pricey. But I miss my family. You have to be careful in case they do a raid. I haven't seen one but I heard…" tongue darting along paper. The blunt sticky from her lip gloss, she said I was a good listener.

Every minute she talked to me I was taking her away from a customer. I slid her a bill at a lull in the conversation.

"I don't like it when they want you to drink with them and you don't want to, and they get angry… really angry. We've had big rappers in here. And big bands after they finish a concert. You tell yourself you're lucky you got here… Are you wearing a miraculous medal? My mom had one... It's $500 for a table in the square."

VI.

I am the owner of a smoothly contoured 2x2cm ellipsoid tumor. Avascular, bloodless like these words, non-calcified unlike my ancestors, palpable and initiated into reality by cautious fingertips.

VII.

"A girl like you doesn't need to do it. Doesn't need to feel sad," the EMT told me thirteen years ago, commuting from the E.R. to the adolescent behavioral ward.

"You have so much going for you, you just need to believe in something." He held my hand and smiled, wrapped me in a white blanket bordered by blue stripes as the ambulance bumped over potholes.

"Jesus loves you," he told me.

"Somebody has to."

VIII.

X sits before me during a meeting. Eyes cast downward, doodling one character after another. Normally faces, men and women, hats or beards, collars or glasses. Before him on the opposite side of the table, my fingers play the keys of my laptop like a piano, hammering letter by letter. I write as a record for myself only. A shallow debrief. No one will have these words. Dry moths cracking apart at the slightest touch.

IX.

My boyfriend was out of town and my neighbor was outside. It started as light conversation. It was cold so he invited me inside. I was lonely, drawing all day and not enthusiastic about my project. Drawing from dawn to dusk without a clear tangible appealing accretion of my efforts. Vainly questing, defacing paper after paper. Supplies and time wasted. A sense of drifting, smoking and drinking outside. Studying the cracked stucco of the building, its invading vegetation and mounting garbage, visual refuse of apathetic landlords.

I lived in this building for years with a man much older than I. Like a failed marriage, you tell yourself: all relationships have their problems: we live in an era where people discard what is broken. But I won't be like that, and when the light burns out, I will check the cabinet but find no bulbs and suffice with darkness.

"I'm unhappy," one may say, pushing a wedge of crumbs aside with damp paper towel on the countertop, followed by, "Fish or steak tonight?"

One develops amnesia for the sake of social cohesion. Sleep to go to work the next day. A Fuck You, said rooms apart under his breath, sinks like a splinter under that same nail peeling cellophane off a microwavable lasagna. All splinters work themselves out with time. Don't leave your sneakers on the counter. Why do you hold your shit in at work all day and then stink up our bathroom? You wait until we're home and stuck together to make it more unbearable. I know but you need to lie still for these ear drops.

"You won't leave, I won't let you," one night he tells you while smoking. The terror of this declaration is lost on you, you've been captive so long. Once you read about saints with the miraculous ability of bilocation: appearing multiple places at once. So, you go to work the next day but a part of you is still hiding in the shadow of the previous night when you're assured you will never escape.

But this night with the neighbor, your partner is out of town. My desires seem to arise without the security of surveillance. A child, normally well-behaved, shoplifting a balloon.

My neighbor invited me inside. Once inside, he said he always had a crush on me. That he thought I had one on him too because of our prolonged eye contact when I'd pass him on my way to work in the morning. I could not recall any of these moments, brief encounters he embroidered with disturbing sincerity. I suspected he was a drug dealer.

I shifted the conversation to the furniture in the room we sat and asked him what would go with him. He was moving out after a split with his girlfriend in their shared apartment.

Weeks prior, this girlfriend left. Her father came from Arizona to help. I saw the father while coming home one evening. Empty beer bottles clustered around his ankles in the grass. He was quite friendly, both he and his daughter professed a liking for me. As the night progressed, she cried in the shoulder of my bathrobe, describing her heartbreak. Girl to girl. Snuggling snot in my fleece leopard-print lapel as I suffered the patient injuries of an angel. Love Thy Neighbor.

A week later, I was sitting alone with the heartbreaker boyfriend on his sofa while my partner was out of town.

"I always had a secret crush on you," he said and leaned forward for a kiss, but I darted away.

He led me upstairs and I removed my clothes, stood in front of the mirror, palms parallel on the wall around the mirror's frame so I could watch myself in all my sudden depravity.

No sex. He hit me. At first, I laughed, unimpressed. He hit me again. Grinding my chin into my shoulder, eyes clenched shut, I muffled my discomfort.

I did not respect him. His arrogance did not correspond to his talent. He demanded obedience without the promise of poetry. He was engorged with his own farce of power. I was not mesmerized. Distracted and bored, the brief midair whir of his hand and that clap against my skin. Object acted upon object. A part of me went elsewhere. To some island that jotted all these details within like broken seashells gathered by a child. A dim ceiling light, the blinking nightstand alarm clock, the discarded sock draped over the chair. Speechless bystanders. Bare walls, thumb tack holes scattered in paint.

Love Thy Neighbor.

Images invade. I have not encased them in words, on paper or aloud until now. I am actively participating in this denial.

He continued to message me after. Lapsed into loneliness, apologizing for 'pestering' me. I was polite. Ambivalent to reveal my true self.

But the truth is: I find all people a pester. An interference, an interruption. None rival my solitude. I am possessive of my isolation. I ask them all, do I like you more than being alone?

Except X who sits before me as I type this in a meeting: unaware he has been married to this memory by my mere writing of it in his presence.

I live alone now. I got away. Moved to the big city. No Daddy.

X.

The table shakes from his eraser. X is doodling a girl during our meeting. A common feature of his graphite expressions. Elven potato shaped heads. Large eyes never looking back at him. Floppy hair. Big bottom lips. A serene expression smooths his mouth like a tranquil spell, a map to his heart only he knows.

Instinctively, intuitively, he sketches a girl almost without looking at her while listening to our meeting. A comfort image he has reincarnated on many paper scraps for however many years. The girl. He will always long for the girl. The person I age further from every day. The girl.

But I am content with the gift of his time. Sitting before X in a dull room. I am no longer begging for his body or his thoughts.

Just having him here, even in silence, is the greatest wish. Anybody can have his body if he chooses to give it: to step inside these disintegrating station wagons. Anybody can have his mind if he chooses to deposit his thoughts in them: for something of the soul is defeated in the transmission of words. But time, even beside X in silence, is the irreversible possession. To have his time feels like an achievement. A lonesome triumph. Our thrumming procession towards death, the ultimate asset of our existence. Time.

X is sitting before me and forfeiting his time. No recovery, no replacement, no refund or exchange. Time. His life and mine, that could end any moment, spent here for a fraction of daylight. The wonderful coincidence of his minutes evaporating beside mine. We sit in silence with no advancement toward my secret fantasy, but I sit here knowing in vampiric glee another day is filed with the legion of ghosts. All my heart is phantoms.

I've learned to suppress some of my longing for him and instead study him like an animal. Once, his sleeve rolled up and the pale raised rivulet of the vein in his wrist made me ache. I study his fingers and the way they convene like blessed apostles around the tip of his pencil. Wide brute nails that imprint in my mind long after I look away. By sight I can know these nails, the ghost of an unborn scenario, the sharp shutter of a nail cutting into me. Without thought, he nudges his mustache with his thumb, and I can feel their short gray bristles sweeping my cheek.

X sits before me in supreme calm, steady hand, gaze lowered. Even in stationary silence, his heathered gray cotton shirt rises and recedes with every breath like a cool wave while he draws. With every breath I share nearby and the glorious coincidence of being alive at the same time with him. That somehow, out of the billions of humans on the planet and billions of years the planet existed, our fragile fleeting organic composites have conspired to coexist side by side. How could this be a random occurrence, like two proximate stars bleating their last dim flicker into breathless space, that we may just happen to know each other. We may just happen to be colleagues. With the minutia of an office and its banal organizational upkeep, we may just happen to stumble nearby. In this cold room. Today. A plot on a line fizzling into nowhere. Two huddled animals with little lungs squeezing between eternities. Am I insane to think this special?

X asks me a question. X says my name without lifting his eyes from his paper while sketching bored during our meeting. The vowels of my name manipulate the muscles of his mouth, syllables granted by my parents' twenty-seven years prior. The syllables of my name force themselves aloud, my name breaks the air from his insides. I've been permitted to live this long for him to say my name. I am lost in this noise.

Out of his lungs, his breath forces my name from the silence, a deep voice that disturbs the air like a mined jewel, spurting acid in the blank isolation of our mundane meeting. The mouth I crave, a trap door to my secret life.

Sins arrive from the heart and blind my judgement like dirty windows. His lips and their chapped epidermis scalded by coffee and slighted by wind, tongue stippled by bitter menthol cough drops, tan lips in this dreary autumn evening, shape themselves to my name. Just for me. Just for a moment. I don't hear his question. A clap in the dark.

XI.

X wanted to take this class. Funder relationships, budgetary outlines, project models, estimates utilized to reference larger belief systems. Crafting persuasive techniques per patron. He is a believer.

He gives me things he finds. On the street, on a shelf, inside a book, on a sidewalk.

Items accidentally discarded. Dropped. Forgotten. Misplaced. He picks them up and gives them to me. The rescuer. A postcard, an engraved bookmark, a cross on the curb.

I found myself researching my secret problem. My lack of eating, my disinterest towards ingesting. He commented once, asking me if I lost weight because I wanted to or because I was letting other things upset me. I laughed it off like I always do.

I found myself researching my secret problem. Not the very secret one, not the one you can't see on the outside, but a problem just the same. I stumbled across different female martyrs. Virgins with breasts torn off. Virgins thrown to lions. Virgins killed for rejecting heathen suitors. Virgins beheaded by fathers. Anorexia Mirabilis, the divine lack of appetite.

XII.

X sits before me. Tattered sleeves, the hem frayed ribbon, pocket sealed with electrical tape. He kept the lights off in the back office, waiting for me to come in. Playing music.

I sat beside him. Neither of us looking at each other. Nobody else around. A lurking sense of losing time.

He never looked at me. I leaned back in my chair and let my curved naked throat show white in the dark as we listened to music.

Once, I danced sleepily with my back turned.

Once, he danced with me and his hand hit mine by accident.

Capitulum Quartum

I.

I found myself researching my problem. The comments from others started out positive.

"You look good."

"What's your secret?"

"Did you do it on purpose?"

"I guess it's hard to feel good about yourself nowadays."

II.

X enjoys withholding things from himself. Brought him food and he let it grow cold. Brought him candy and it lay on his desk unwrapped. Brought him two bananas. He only has one.

III.

X sits before me.

The girls. Always drawing girls. Who are these girls? With their small pouting mouths and baby fat cheeks and interfering bangs? Never looking directly at him. Girls.

I can dispense with my time and labor without dispensing my heart. They are trinkets, mayflies that live for a day.

I live for the way X bit his lip as we discussed the Pharisees.

I live for the way X shyly nods when I ask if he left a gift on my desk.

I live for his fingers over mine when I hand him his coffee.

I live to hear the squish of his old sneakers on the tile and the soft knock on my door. I will not turn until he knocks, even if I hear him, I will not turn until he wants me to know he is there.

There's a disorienting fragility to our friendship. I withhold information about myself, I don't think he's as interested in me. I extract more joy from knowing him.

I wish I could know how he breathes when he orgasms. I wish I could feel my ass clench around his thumb nail. To taste the juices dormant in his trousers.

IV.

I've entered a new life I've chosen for myself. A spaghetti dinner night. A book club. Socials. Dances. Bible study. Praying together. It felt good to be wanted and treated with kindness. I told a friend about the warmth and generosity I was experiencing at church, and they said:

"Of course they're nice to you, they think they have a live one."

At first, your friends thought you were joking about church. Then they looked at you like you were abducted by aliens and called you brainwashed while alluding to pederasty.

At church, getting up from the floor hurts your knees more than the floor. You come to find the pain a cleansing participant that enriches your concentration on the altar.

V.

"I'm going to sign here, date and time. I need you to do the same," the doctor says without making eye contact as the elderly Latina nurse lines up needles on a napkinned tray with blue Latex hand.

"I'm going to walk you through every step, it will be a short procedure," she says this like a phone operator. Every sentence recited in bloodless timbre. There is nothing reassuring or incriminating. She examines women's insides like steaming cappuccinos. She is not permitted to tell you the truth currently. She only directs. You lie back, clutching your miraculous medal like the virgin self you hurried to discard fourteen years ago.

"I've situated the microscope. I'm going to spray a vinegar solution that will react with abnormal cells."

And you light up like a Christmas tree. Like a thousand stars in the vacuum of space. Like a blood spatter under blue wand. And you feel her faint nudge, like a cold penny, deep inside you.

"Do you see abnormal cells?" you ask.

"Yes, I need to do three biopsies minimum."

The ceiling is neutral, lukewarm milk, your only witness. The doctor finishes and tells you to sit up, get yourself together, the nurse will check on you in five minutes.

"We didn't get answers, but we got information," the doctor says like a forensic profiler. She can investigate you with a dispassionate gaze and know you are just a sheep on the lower plain. A sick creature pecked off.

You hurry on your clothes. Your combat boots come on tighter than expected.

Somehow, the awful irony creeps into you. Of that fat man at work waddling to the pizza parlor on his lunch break, a man whose face exhibits a state of total desolation when you tell him: I haven't had a single French fry in over a year. That fat man may outlive you now.

Whore. Girls can't act like boys.

VI.

"Ladies and gentlemen of the jury, please stay seated until I instruct otherwise. The defendant is charged with homicide."

The wave of unreality sets in, my fingers comb the fresh, shorn hairs on my scalp and seconds evaporate. What if I were to faint, beating breathless and cold in a room of eighty strangers.

"If you objected to participation due to moral reasons from the death penalty, please note this option is not present for this case."

The judge had trouble reading off the names of lab experts, hyphenated and foreign.

"Good morning, everyone," the accused murderer said, yellow flannel shirt, nodding.

What do two gunshot wounds to the chest spray at what length? Close contact exit wounds at what caliber barrel?

"How long have you lived in this city?" the judge asked me. My eyes drifted down, trying to remember the years I lived off the radar like a perverted ward to an older man.

"Dismissed."

VII.

Once, two years before, when I lived with this man, we were arguing. Before I lived alone in this city, talking to this judge. I was opening the fridge, and the man told me if I didn't listen to him and stay, that he would call the police on me. I laughed and replied:

"What will you tell them? Oh, help me Mr. Policeman, my girlfriend is trying to leave.

Please Mr. Policeman, won't you help? Mr. Policeman, please Mr. Policeman…" and he shoved me into the fridge from behind, my robe knocking magnets off the freezer to the floor.

VIII.

Tonight: A Ziploc bag with your laundry change, quarters meant to clean your clothes, you head to the corner store to buy box mac and cheese because you could've sworn you had a box, prepared to have a box, thought you had a box, no meat on Friday. But you were wrong and noticed at 9pm.

You take your bag of laundry change with you, hoping somewhere will be open. A delivery boy on a bicycle darts in front of you on the sidewalk, "They should know they can't be here. You know how many times I was almost killed by one of them. You know how many times I was almost killed by a car?" a skinny middle-aged man pleads in your ear as the automatic doors part.

You walk to the dry goods aisle. Oatmeal, crackers, apple sauce. You find the cheapest mac and cheese. $5.19. Food harder to buy, you cut down on what you enjoyed, but even the simple stuff is hard. You know you only have $5.00 in laundry quarters in your pocket. It's all you have until pay day next week. Instead of turning back you head to the registers.

All closed, use self-checkout. No chance at human sympathy. You are left with a metal sensor bagging area, a camera with blown out pixels. With shameful precision, you deposit each quarter slowly. You know you won't reach the limit, but this rehearsal is necessary. One quarter doesn't read, you must drop it twice. And then you watch the digits blink backward. $4.94 $4.69… $4.44…

Your throat is tightening with tears, you knew you wouldn't have enough money before you came to the register. You were pretending the entire way.

At the self-check next to you, the man who jostled you at the entrance, the despiser of cyclists, completes his transaction and you hear a dozen coins clatter in the knee-high bin.

"I um… I need my money back… I am short," you tell the employee laughing with another employee. You are one quarter short for a box of mac and cheese. You are not making eye contact. You are clenching your teeth.

"Oh, I got you," he says and gives you one quarter. It completes the transaction. You get six cents back and hand it to the employee with your receipt.

"What's your name?" you ask him.

"Dave."

"I'll pray for you, Dave."

"It's just a quarter."

IX.

Dear Mr. Policeman,

She'll go to hell if she does it. She knows that before the rest of us. We've discovered her lunch hours run over while going to the Catholic church around the corner. Yes, Mr. Policeman, we thought she was Jewish too. She did something like this once years ago, but we don't really remember. Mr. Policeman, we didn't expect this from her. Maybe from the others, the newer ones. It's our fault, Mr. Policeman, we didn't check on this. There were signs.

She would hide the paper she was writing on when we entered the room. We never saw her eat. She hardly spoke of herself. She was giving exorbitantly to charities. Mr. Policeman, we thought this was one of her charming naïve traits, to love to the point of denial. We should really check in on everyone, Mr. Policeman. If it could happen to her who knows for the others.

X.

The bartender has smoky gray hair like a Puritan and knows more about you than you've told him. The first time you met him he looked grim, lean and looming behind the bar. Herman Munster tall.

He didn't like you because you didn't have cash. You were just another girl shouting an order over music. He was your boss's best friend but neither of you knew this at the time. Leaning on the wood he'd epoxied himself, a counter you would wipe down with a rag one year later. Under him.

You returned to this same bar a year later after learning who he was. The bartender had gleaming eyes when he realized who you were as well. He'd also been hearing of you for quite some time.

You returned. After you were done being blonde. Done having a boyfriend. Penniless and alone. Your drinks were free that night.

The bartender invited you to work for him, a favor to his friend to help you out. At your first gig, you were assigned a bar by a fireplace on the second floor. You were eager and overly polite. This made you appear even more new. He showed you things without your asking. How to unlock the cabinets with a key he never gave anyone. How to make a layered sweet drink with a fancy spiraled spoon. You thought it was just another lesson. Until he smiled and asked you to drink it with him.

"It tastes like candy," he said.

"It's delicious," you replied.

Watching couples laughing. Smiling with approving warmth at a young man dancing with an old woman, blushing from her chardonnay.

"What do you love about your job?" you asked him while drying a glass. He seemed surprised, like nobody'd asked him this before.

"Every night's a party," he answered.

The cognac was unexpected. At the end of the shift. Just the two of you after everyone left. Caterers tossing smocks in a hamper, checks cut, tips divided. After you washed all the glasses, carried the mop to the basement. A mop larger than you. Counting all the liquor caps.

The cognac was unexpected. His quick large hands had a painterly confidence while pouring. You didn't notice what he was doing until the shot glasses were full. He asked you to have it with him. You got down eye level with the glass and laughed. Nervous about your small unfed frame drinking cognac at 2am with the bartender.

He walked you home, saying he had to buy cigarettes, but you knew he already had some. You struggled with the gate upon leaving. Black wrought iron, leaning your shoulder into it but it wouldn't budge. He told you to growl at it. You did as he directed and he opened it for you.

On the short walk to your apartment, he stepped over a bum sleeping face down on the sidewalk, handfuls of pound cake strewn across a steaming manhole.

"They call him Little Feather One-Shoe." the bartender snickered at the bum's bare foot.

XI.

Dear Mr. Policeman,

We never had an issue with her before. On occasion her supervisor expressed concern for her lack of vacation time. Reliable, this word arises half a dozen times in her annual performance review. Impressive, bright future ahead. Always enlisting in professional development programs, team building exercises. Communicative, she always consults her supervisor and colleagues about any changes to workflow or anticipated action. This situation comes as a surprise to us all. She is never like this. Mr. Policeman, we have an address on file. We know she's the artistic type, maybe she got flustered. It's not unheard of, with the stress going around. Maybe she'll reach out. Let's give her the benefit of the doubt, Mr. Policeman.

The burn out quiz we provided all staff charted her cortisol levels as moderate, suspended atop the fence of healthy and inordinate stress. And that's where she lies, ladies and gentlemen of the jury. A dot affixed in the middle of the plane. A single isolated center surrounded by unnamed ether.

Capitulum Quintum

I.

"I saw his car in the driveway when I got home from work, but he was allowed to come and go as he pleased," my aunt explained while sipping iced water. My mother insisted on hearing her recollection of events. My mother wanted the complete story. Always the detective.

We all pretended not to notice my aunt crying silently on the sofa as we mingled with each other. In our black clothing, holding paper plates but never eating. The dog curled up to my aunt and began to snore. A friend of my uncle's approached me. A little man with a drug problem, placed his hand on my arm, gazing at my black lace gloves, admiring my veil, handmade rosary and velvet dress. I figured, when I awoke that morning for my uncle's funeral, that he would want me to pull out all the stops. He would want his niece to appear, in all glorious gothic attire, for his funeral. He would want every operatic detail, every stitch of eyelash lace seared to the flesh, sobbing and smearing mascara. And this little man with the drug problem, my uncle's friend, touched my arm and told me:

"I know this is a funeral and this will sound inappropriate, but you are totally killing it."

A successful audition.

Sometimes I can't sleep because I think I hear my aunt screaming.

She's grunting through the doorway from some vague indigestion, kicking off her orthopedic clogs next to the dog water bowl. And there is my uncle on the sofa. Still as a gargoyle. Some obliterated shell with blood everywhere. And she screams because his face is blown apart like spaghetti.

Sometimes it doesn't feel like he killed himself. Like he died from natural causes that were natural unto himself. Because he was always crazy. Like there wasn't anything unnatural about how he died. At his own hands by firearm. Like he was just obeying the natural conclusion of his lifelong pathological biome.

But he loved me. With those eyes glittering on me before I noticed him. Telling me I was beautiful.

I see her coming home from work. My aunt. Putting her handbag on the yellow Formica kitchen counter. Rubbing her forehead against an oncoming migraine. Coughing. And she shuffles into the living room.

This is where I lose the details. She runs to him out of panic. Or she thinks he's just injured himself. Or she smirks suspecting he's faking it, waiting there, leaning back in the sofa with his hands on his chest like Cleopatra, holding his breath for her flurry of concern. Or maybe she notices him from the doorway, in silent doe-like terror. Waiting for a snapped twig or pulled trigger, that maybe if we walk in and nobody touches a thing, this didn't happen. She creeps into the musty living room like a hellish museum. Like she's setting afoot some desert planet. She walks toward him. Inspecting and cautious. Like maybe, just maybe, if you don't make a sound, it may all just be a dream. One more close call.

But he loved me. On that park bench years before, my uncle told me, in an admission of private resignation, that in fact my dear niece, please listen: every passing car you see has a radio in it the military is signaling that hears everything we say. He looked at the ground after telling me this, a solemn pause while absorbing the true sorrow of this fact. But my uncle loved me and decided to tell me the truth, that I was worth the risk of bodily harm, to protect me at his own expense. In sad reflection, he considered the jeopardy he'd put us both in by telling me this, but chose to continue:

"I'm sorry to be the one to tell you this, but we're not safe anymore. What are you pretending not to know? Because the sign is getting bigger every day."

I saw it then, the shadow of what my mother warned me about. That once he stood naked in a window of a Las Vegas high rise about to jump and old ladies screamed on the sidewalk below.

My mother seemed to think he and I could mend each other, that I could pull him back from the ledge. We both had mental hospitals in common. But he loved me.

My uncle is on the sofa.

Strangely he didn't ruin the walls, according to my aunt.

I look at his pictures now more than I ever did. He blew a hole the diameter of a soda can above his right ear. I'm uncertain if knowing his face stayed intact is a consolation while looking at his pictures.

Sometimes I wonder about the final day. If he felt some covert victory as he pumped gas in his car, with that pistol in his belt. Or maybe while clicking the nozzle, his eye strayed to the glove compartment, housing some femme fatale. And maybe life's little wounds that day slid off him. Finding at last, power in detachment. My mother always said he felt too much.

Maybe the calm resolve cured the daily aches. Being cut off in traffic, the doldrum line at the pharmacy, the squeaky wheel of the shopping cart erring too far left. The halfway house, the men's house, and now at last, the narrowest house underground.

I used to see the wall and hear the gunshot. But now I don't hear my aunt screaming anymore, in my mind's uncontrollable eye. The sounds I imagined trying to sew together what happened, mute themselves like settling dust. Instead, I hear what actually happened, my aunt sniffling on the sofa. None of us acknowledge her tears, we won't interfere with her grieving.

And my mother is next to her, the unshakable detective half-blind in her walker, asking my aunt endless questions. My mother, who through every calamity or confusion demands answers. To survive on the truth. To withstand the withering merciless gusts of life, wants a place on the map. My mother wants clear tangential coordinates for her brother's despair.

"Were there signs?" My mother prods.

My mother wants a narrative arc charting culpability. Accounting misfortunes whose onset may be espied like malignant cells or enemy encampments for extermination.

"Where were you? How did you find him? What did you do?" My mother asks my aunt because the police wouldn't tell her.

My mother wants a definitive point on the ledger of infinity that articulates our place in the chaos. She wants to locate her brother in the rip tide.

My mother wants an answer. With its sharp shredding teeth and unfailing autopsies that go to the coroner for one to three business days before being released to the funeral home.

No uncertainties allowed, even for the man who took the truth with him. And no matter how much we try to exorcise the doomed patterns of my uncle's life, he will always take first place as his biggest critic.

II.

The bartender has strange hands, "bar rot" another server described, a junkie missing half his leg from being shoved out a window, who likewise quipped to be, "young, dumb, and full of cum."

The bartender's hands, nightly submerged in frost blue sanitizer water, have nails ribbed and round. Grendel gnarled. But you'd just as easily let them unbutton your blouse you bought on discount for his job. Whore to the core.

"When's church tomorrow?" he asks you without looking up from a glass, rubbing away a pink crescent of lipstick.

III.

I see that picture. My aunt and uncle on a hayride. On his shoulder is a camera the size of a sewing machine. The sensitive chronicler. My aunt's head is cocked to the side as if she's listening for the gun shot that would blow his head off twenty years later. In the picture he's laughing, and the girl is still a baby and doesn't hate him yet. Her matted wet lashes at the funeral, as she told me in the living room cramped with strangers, that I was always her favorite cousin.

I wish I could tell her I'm not the one.

She said she wanted to be just like me when she grew up. I squeezed my cigarettes in my purse and smiled kind and curious, thanking her. I cannot agree with her aloud because all I see is my skinny adolescent arms holding her on my hip on the boardwalk as a toddler, her blonde ringlets catching the neon sign of the ice cream shop.

Children ever watchful and yearning, eyes gleaming green orbs absorbing my every fickle fain and mundane pitch. My blind teenage rage enchanting a child whose parents were high some state away. And then I hear the gunshot.

IV.

"I feed about ten guys a night. And I'm talking guys way gone. Not like me," the bum tells me as his flat hand sails out from the orange bandana on his forehead to the traffic light ahead. I'm standing under him on the hot sidewalk, buildings tall gray looming like headstones, a summer storm about to come through. He's a bum I see every day on my corner.

"Where you get it? The food you give the other guys?" you ask, "Is it all the orders people buy from these fancy food places but don't pick up?" and he nods at you.

You both grin. Being broke here, with the heat therapy yoga studios and by-appointment tailors, is like being at a buffet with your hands tied. Endless window shopping. You pass bars, bistros, restaurants, pubs, clubs, boutiques and parlors, with a diaphragm disengaged. A stomach that only growls for water. Shoes that rub a little too close to the cement.

You know this guy you're talking to has been out all day. You speak to him almost every day. Some days you can't approach him, he sits with his guitar on a milk crate outside an auto-open storefront, raking chords. Once he told you he would get a place real soon, wouldn't be out here much longer.

Sometimes you walk by and ask if he needs anything, sometimes he says no while smiling. Sometimes he wants cereal. Or headphones. Or underwear. You've spoken to this man about a year but didn't learn his name until a week ago, Jerry.

Ten minutes before you run into Jerry you come down a sidewalk and pause in front of a fancy shop window. You admire the setup, a blue and orange tiger-striped silk sofa. A nearby nightstand with crystal tumblers and plastic ice cubes inside. A mannequin in a nightgown stands by the sofa. No gunshots here.

A mannequin stands there, just thin enough, that one may discern the sharp hip bone jutting forward from its satin night gown.

You stand on the sidewalk staring at the mannequin. Broke and hungry, in childlike imitation, you lace your fingers across your chest and thrust out your hip just like the mannequin.

Your reflection in the shop window vanishes because there is no longer glass dividing you. There are no more pissed off balding businessmen detouring around your frozen frame on the sidewalk, cursing past curbside parking meters, annoyed at your sidewalk tryst with this mannequin.

You and this mannequin are square. One on one. Mano a mano, equals inside out. You look just as good. In your isolation. In your hunger. In your loneliness on this hot day.

You both dance a fair game together. You and this mannequin. Your bodies willfully brutalized to be sylph-like. Pursuing pixies, ageless and evading captivity. To be a fairy. Lighter than air. They can't catch a shadow. They can't get you when you're nowhere to be found.

You're a soldier in a movement towards reduction, a serious statement of period resistance. You are abstaining, lending weight to convictions of losing weight. Shedding oneself to the core. Distilling yourself to your purest elements. Defying and demolishing every expectation of your body. Discarding all detritus and dimorphic sarcophagi of previous selves. You have no body. A body the doctors imply may kill you.

You will flatten every curve. You will neutralize every inch. You will shrink inward, centimeter by centimeter. You will measure every fractional adjustment toward invisibility like a ritual. The pink tape measure in your backpack is a trophy over every private failure.

With godlike resolve, through kenosis and ketosis, in mutual bondage, your body will get smaller. Even someone, as innocuous and unassuming as an old lady by an elevator, will want to touch you, as she tries to squeeze by. People will tell you how good you look. And you will forfeit everything.

We are a diagram, not a body. We are rare superficial squamous epithelium cells that alight under vinegar solution. You are fighting the pollution of predilections for micro-foam lattes. But the thoughts still plague you. Those thoughts of longing.

The chewy center of a salted fudge brownie. The slick buttery trail of a noodle in the corner of my mouth. The pillowy center of a pancake pressed into a warm pool of syrup. The crisp crumble of a burnt cookie on my blouse. Food haunts me. I sit in the park and watch three girls on a blanket open a pizza box. Cheese stretching over their wrists.

The scale is a fickle whore. I only consult her when I feel like we have the same aim. I account for every calorie dispensed on equipment and ingested nightly, but I am becoming helpless in the face of numbers. A scale. A treadmill. A mathematical equation for a night class consisting of Greek letters with exponents in parenthesis over fractions being squared. Ancient Sanskrit to my confused eyes, the stitching in my mask rips. The emails aggregate. My bank account shrinks. Then my diagnosis. Time stands still. I can't move. I can't get up out of myself. I lose all numbers. I become one.

The new priest, who smiles brightly and stands too close to your face while speaking, enters your mind and says:

"Our bodies have a fair gage of when they're fed. More or less. Sometimes there's a lag of a couple minutes. Our hearts are not the same. They don't always know when they're fed. And you're not yourself when you're hungry."

And you are hungry. You sell half the clothes in your closet. You bartend. But you can be this mannequin if you want, that stops you on the sidewalk in broad daylight. The mannequin you halt for mid-step and ogle while strangers slip around you like parting platelets sliding toward the park. The skinny mannequin in the nightgown in the smashed shop window, you watch her behind the glass like she will talk to you like a sister. Like she will dare you further. She stands behind an orange and blue tiger-striped silk sofa in the rich downtown neighborhood you despise because you can't join. Because in the morning you don't have money for coffee but can look up and admire the potted plants in their bay windows. Because the only things you can control in this life are your love for God and your body. No other dreams permitted.

But you were half right, and your life will be half as long, as the doctor describes next steps. Lasers. Excisions.

V.

"Who do you think you got it from?" your mother asks on the phone.

"I don't know, why would you ask that?"

"So I know who to park my car on top of," your mother replies.

Harry, Steve, Nathan, Nick, Jake, Jack, Raymond, Daniel, David, Dominic, Josh, Jonah.

Strand 16, 18, 31, 33, 35, 39, 45, 51, 52, 56, 58, 59, 66, 68.

They never say what strand. Except three are the worst.

They never remember you. Them, the boys and men, as they sip beer and watch the game. Maybe they have kids by now.

VI.

They're gonna steal your skinny. With that New Superdrug. Like a pandemic. You saw a laminated flyer for it on the back of the door in the doctor's office. Before the test you insisted on. An ad on the door. The new skinny drug.

At the doctor's office, their questions are more thorough and deliberate than before. Suddenly they want the dates of certain things. They want descriptions of menses, viscous flow, day to day. They do depression screenings, mundane inquiries. Are you finding yourself less interested in things you used to enjoy? They double check your weight. They double check your height. You lie on the pleather mat with a paper blanket over your knees and the doctor that comes in wants you to sit up and asks if you're alright. They are checking your weight on the clipboard but say nothing.

The doctor talks to you like she's reading a brunch menu. Cheddar stuffed biscuits. Abnormal cell production. Caramel snickerdoodles. Persistent infection.

You realize that in the future, you won't have to try so hard to be skinny anymore.

VII.

It's everywhere, first it started with your friend and then it spread to your mother. The New Superdrug. They liked to sit at the table too long after the meal. Then the needle came along every few days. The pounds slid off and they admitted a general malaise. The New Superdrug arrived during your great quest, the great movement towards reduction. They bought their thinness with that New Superdrug like their chicken combo. Your mother and friend articulate an overall disregard for food, only managing a bite. This makes you envious. To be so devoid of desire seems like a dream.

They square their meals with the needle. And you start to hate it. This drug on the news. The drug celebrities take. The drug that invaded your home. They get skinny without suffering like you did. They bought their perfection. In line at the pharmacy, shoulder nudging cheap rack bifocals to synth pop. They're going to take your skinny away.

But there's that one morning, you stood holding a coffee in the back office, trying to explain to X, why you loved heroin chic fashion.

You said, without flinching, our enchantment with the emaciated figure originates from a subconscious fixation on depictions of Christ. And you said, eyes riveted upon an unknown point in space, that to be so thin, was to take on all feeling in the world and become distilled. To be carved down to an essential undefeatable core.

They're gonna steal your skinny. Everything's for sale.

VIII.

The GrandAna online has many tips as follows:

- ✓ Never tell anyone. Even people you trust, people acting out of goodwill can say whatever they want when they're loaded on moral authority. And then they'll put you away, for your own good they'll say. And then you've lost forever.
- ✓ Ana girls are strong. They fight dizzy spells. And if you must binge, revert to fudgesicles at 40 calories a pop. Easy to purge, doesn't hurt like celery or carrots.

- ✓ Wear a rubber band on your wrist. When the hunger invades, give the band a hard slap against your skin. The sharp sting will merge the yearning for food with an unwelcome sensation.
- ✓ Put your fork down after every bite and count every chew. Never eat past 7pm.
- ✓ Clean something disgusting. The moldy black grime around your shower mat, the calcified deposits rimming your sink faucet, the underside of the toilet seat spotted with fecal stains. The sight of the crusted result of eating and the harsh smell of bleach will make all savory fantasies subside.
- ✓ Diet soda, the caffeine will make you smile more.
- ✓ Brush your teeth if you're hungry. Won't want to defile that minty mouth.

- ✓ Glass of water before every meal. Apple after every glass of water. Then wait fifteen minutes.
- ✓ Good posture burns calories. Any movement at all is good. Wiggle your foot. And if you're cold, make yourself colder. Wear that camisole in winter. Being cold makes your body burn more calories.
- ✓ Put them at ease, they will wonder like idle minds do. Buy a salad sans dressing/croutons at a fast-food drive thru and leave the empty paper bag in crumpled glory on top of the trash can. They'll think you left your trash out, readily visible in thoughtless indulgent display.
- ✓ When you buy clothes, get them a size too small. Something to aim for, a reward for yourself.

The GrandAna emphasizes we must not neglect personal pampering. Paint your nails and do a mud mask. This is a slow serious descent. Embrace this private drama with kabuki gusto, unending poetry for your prison. A body supine like an Etruscan widow on your bed sheets. Stunning solitary ice sculpture.

And they've started to touch me more than they ever did. Strangers and acquaintances. Small talk and they place their hand on your back without provocation. The nape of your neck cradled by their hand, jokingly aggressive. An elbow suddenly ushered over a threshold by intrigued fingertips. A man in line at the grocery store wants to tap your shoulder. You need a guiding hand on your sharp bones.

Who may deny the languid enchantment of a pallid arm, gossamer thin, poised midair above a stapler? Pale neck taut like a slim candle.

"We are body-soul composites," the young priest declares, "in our fragile human neediness, we require tokens of this world to remind us of the uncharted world beyond."

Father draws a eucharist in streaky blue marker on a whiteboard. You listen from your slat back chair in the last row as the local high school band practices the Indiana Jones theme song in the adjoining rec hall of this church basement.

Body. Soul. Composite.

IX.

"Let's go to the river," the bartender said. Your phone was dead, and you made a joke about it: that if he cut you up into chum and tossed you to the fish, nobody would know a thing. You whispered this and he laughed with his lips hovering over your neck, on the sidewalk in the orange island of light from a streetlamp.

At the river's edge, the winking broken triangles of bridge lights covered your powdered cheeks in a sad wan dew. Distant cars honking and ambulance sirens ringing faint like inner city evening tinsel. A cyclist passed and you noticed the bartender's hand cupping your hip. His chin smooth from shaving, resting on your shoulder.

You kiss the small piercing hole under his bottom lip and admire the teenager who did it. You have him now at the black water's edge, with his silver helmet of hair and unbuttoned shirt, the bartender, but for a minute you're sitting with that football player that pierced his own lip in the school bathroom on a dare.

"Kids are dumb they'll do anything to their bodies," he says, before you pull him down to the grass. The doctors make you wonder if you'll die so now you wrestle life to the ground.

And he sits in a chair in your apartment later and wordlessly swallows your crazed stare, as you stand with bare backside against the oven door.

He's colorblind so you ask him, just to be cruel, "What color are my eyes?" and shut them.

"Clear like water."

Body. Soul. Composite.

X.

"I just don't get it," your father says on the phone, "I never heard of anyone becoming Catholic. I heard of people who used to be Catholic but nobody becoming Catholic. Like nobody moves to Ohio, they move from Ohio."

At the baptism, they fit you for a white robe and you receive a Youth Male Age 10-12. And they tell you that tonight will be the night you die. Let your old self die away and confess one baptism.

Your Jewish father is squinting at you from his pew, as you bend over the well, like he's on another planet. Your mother can't stop her reflux cough.

X is sitting in a pew in the middle of the church, serious and silent. His face stone. You see him leave the church at the end of the service at midnight, and you watch him cross himself in the arched doorway, and there is something violent and dutiful in the swift clip of his elbow. Like a soldier.

The water is ice cold on your forehead from its metal crib. They give you a towel and you can't walk straight.

And you did just that, you threw down your nets, like Simon and Andrew at the shore, and walked with Him. Your ancestors ran into the woods and climbed up trees hiding from pogroms. All your mother wanted was to raise good Jewish children. Your grandfather sang Yiddish in the car ride to Hebrew school. You had a Bat Mitzvah. You could even say the Mourner's Kaddish in Hebrew when your uncle shot himself.

"You're a traitor, you took the side of the Spanish Inquisition," a friend suggested. You betrayed your Ashkenazi heritage, clinging to their shawls and clenching their jaws against raging Russian blizzards, exchanged for the silent rocking of the bronze incense thurible patching smoke down the aisle.

You pray your rosary in Latin. You make rosaries with chain and semi-precious stones and give them to the local convent. The blisters on your palms from pliers and wire cutters are hardening into thick yellow callouses. A pouting Midwestern missionary with stringy brown hair holds a rosary you made, her fingers dipping between gapped beads, and asks you with solemn gravity, "Do you realize you're making weapons?"

And you stand on that scale, holding your hair back behind your ears with hesitant hands at sunrise, looking down at the digits. And the bartender gropes you just a little too hard that night. Like he expects more to be there. His hand comes away half full, but you feel like you gave him everything.

XI.

I confess, to Almighty God, and to you my brothers and sisters, that I have greatly sinned. In my thoughts and in my words, in what I have done and what I have failed to do.

Your head knocks against the wall as the bartender bites your neck. You have rug burn on your back. You cannot tell him the shadows that live in your body.

"Dirty slut," he calls you as he grips your ponytail. That gnarled hand submerged in blue topaz sanitizer water that night, watching everyone dance while suds drift down the lip of a rocks glass.

The poetry invades, how your bodies twirled about each other behind that bar he epoxied himself. Passing him a glass, uncorking a bottle, snapping a lid, cleaving ice with a metal scoop. The thoughtless melody of your movements cramped behind the counter. How you heaved hauling an orange bucket of ice upstairs. Your bodies circle each other like doomed planets, careening in orbital ease around a belt loop, around a trash can. And then you know the little sprouts of hair around his nipples and that dim dotted ring on your neck has his mouth everywhere at once.

You straddle him and think of how tall and morose he seemed behind that bar the first time you saw him. Your chain bracelets swinging around your thin wrist as you picked up your drink. You think of the sly charm in his eye which has now softened dark, forest green, and dares to tell you:

"I'm nervous."

XII.

It's a Jubilee Year according to the Church. A time of reconciliation and renewal every twenty-five years. On this occasion, the relics of St. Thomas Aquinas experienced an intercontinental passage. Traversing oceans, skipping time zones, the relics of St. Thomas Aquinas are visiting my church from France. One site of a select few on the East coast. The first time his relics have come to the United States, 750 years after his death.

Standing in the last pew by the exit, his skull arrived in a hand painted box on silk pillow on a bronze lectica. Four long pole handles rest atop the shoulders of four men. His skull was brown, and I waited until after the service, to walk up to it and kneel on the brick floor. With my mouth shut and hands clasped at chest, I stared into his empty black sockets and heard a whizz behind my head like a hot iron. Head pulsing, I'm pulled into the invisible gaze of a saint and asking what it returns.

Capitulum Sextum

I.

My fixation on hands is lifelong. As a girl I imagined a hundred men lined up. Covered in black robes, long sleeves, heavy hoods concealing their faces, and all I could see were their hands. That I would go down the line, man by man, and inspect every hand. I would review every digit and contour of crooked bone. It would not be until I found the man with the perfect hands that I could surrender my search. He could be a brute, mongrel, or madman, but my fate would be sealed by the hands.

On a bench at dusk, I found myself running my thumb over the bartender's hands. Nails ribbed and edges blunted, heavy plum tips stained by tobacco. A deep betrayal of my lifelong fantasy of perfection. Hands deformed by decades of rough labor, teethed by wood and mottled brick. Sensitive to every tap and touch of my own. Matching my every twitch and tingle and covering me like a shadow.

II.

Desire found me. Not where I was waiting, around the corner, on a bend, by a bench, waiting. Not buying coffee, combing my bangs before entering a room. Not over my shoulder as I stood on a scale at sunrise, my cold thin feet sucking glass, scribbling down decimals on a notepad. Not listening for his footsteps, no, this is not where desire found me.

Desire found me when I spent most of my life looking the other way. Expecting to die. Jumping out of planes. Desire came like a wolf in the face of a neighbor that greeted me on a street corner. As I stood in shorts and flip flops at a stoplight, holding a case of beer on my birthday. No one I suspected. The least I expected.

Desire came strange and sullen like a teenager, glaring at caterers zipping by with trays of empty champagne flutes. Tall and silent. Vested in black with long gray hair pulled back like a pilgrim. Giving me extra shifts as a favor to his friend.

And then desire appeared in ambivalent adolescent blows. Dingey blue jeans sauntering down my street as I stood on the sidewalk, curling my toes in my shoes.

Desire found me when it started to get cold. When the only people left in the park were bellhops walking poodles for the nearby hotel. It found me when we didn't know what to say to each other and pulled on our cigarettes we both wanted to quit. And he said he was homeless at seventeen, living out of his car that his parents confiscated from a motel parking lot.

Two men entered my mind at that moment. I saw him, before I was even born, his gray locks enlivened brown, a skinny seventeen-year-old boy waking up and lifting the blinds of his motel room that morning. A motel room he got for one lucky night. Checking on his car, no family, no friends. Living in his car when other kids were packing up their parents' station wagons with pillows and duffle bags for dorm floors. His fingers lift those blinds, eyes blearily register the terror to see: no car. There is just the heartless black outline of asphalt rimmed by fresh snow. One night's sleep and no rest forever.

And then another man enters my mind. The man sitting on this bench with me, arm around my shoulder, telling me this like it's nothing. His hand heavy on my knee like a dry grizzled paw.

And I hand him a rose I bought after work, and he says he wants to drop it off at his place. I am hurt, like he doesn't want to be seen with it, but then he tells me, "I don't think anyone's given me a rose before."

I couldn't relax when he held me. It terrified me to be still in his arms with my eyes shut. In my mind, I recited my Hail Mary eight times, my Nicene Creed, Apostle's Creed, Gloria, Hail Holy Queen, the Fatima, Saint Michael, and Saint Rita, asking God to bless this man who'd been to every state except Hawaii, with a horrific scar on his knuckle and dark eyes that only stared at me when I wasn't looking back.

My sister told me I was a walking Freudian nightmare when I told her how old he was. My boss became curt and cold. And suddenly, with the bartender, I found him to tend many things. Plants. Windows. Children. That somehow, he had tended me.

III.

Twenty-nine and a teenager again. You kiss the splinter he got yesterday moving a table. A unique joy overcomes you, to imagine him leaning over that table, as if it were you, and the sudden bite of wood into his hand, that hand that entered you the day before. And the way he ferociously pinches blood from the welt under a running faucet.

His room is soundproof, and you don't ask why. You look at his face in the dim blue light and can't tell if it's a smile. But he rushes you out, someone is coming over sooner than expected with friends. And for a second you confuse your belt for his on the bed. And your face is red raw because he didn't shave. He greeted you earlier at the front door, barefoot nonchalant bohemian, to take you up three flights of stairs to show you the catwalk.

A fire exit with a narrow-suspended walkway between buildings, the skyscrapers seem prettier here. Alone in the heart of dense urban migraine. Everyone far below on this chilly September night, and you stand suspended together on this overhead fire escape, two solitary silhouettes like rogue angels. You go out on the catwalk and turn to him and ask him why he is showing you all of this. And he looks at you surprised, like you just don't get it.

He clips his belt quickly while keeping a cigarette in his mouth. He even remembers the water bottle you left on the floor. You can't leave a trace. He tells you later he's sorry for rushing you out.

And you laugh off your hurt and tell him it's like you're fifteen again, an amused tart.

You skip down the hall of your building to your door and mutter to yourself, "If you're going to act like a whore you're going to be treated like one."

IV.

Your bag clanks against the glass store front at night, back nudging the hours sign. He kisses your ear, sucking on the lobe with a single pearl earring.

"Watch out, you swallow my earring, and you'll turn into an oyster," you say. He asks if they're real and you decline. Somewhere, hidden behind the cataract of overcast sky, there is a supermoon swelling with autumn harvest.

V.

He calls you from a rest stop and you can hear the cough and growl of trucks in the back. He's clicking a gas nozzle, blanketed by some strange interstate darkness, asking you about your day in short, perfunctory manner.

And you can know, through the phone, how his hair feels when you tug it, and you pinch the phone to your jaw.

"My day was fine, went to church, went to the gym,"

"I'll call you tomorrow," he says.

Earlier, you raged on the treadmill, hoping to avoid hoping for his call that promises a call another night.

Capitulum Septimum

I.

Rosh Hashana, the Jewish New Year, and you run to the train but still miss it. Your family is expecting you, even though they think you've forgotten everything from your upbringing since becoming Catholic. You wait an hour for the next train, the day is gray, and life seems to be getting to everyone as the world turns over on its side midsleep toward autumn. Your boss is lamenting the world that never cut him a break, and he's giving you the side eye since you started seeing the bartender.

The train to the suburbs is overcrowded, you stand forty minutes with a heavy brown bag of food.

Your mom called you three times and texted you demanding you call her immediately. She says, "Will you buy the challah, your father had a rough month."

You received communion in your hands today, not on your knees per daily practice. You just couldn't kneel yourself before the calamities. First, they come like one bird. Then two. And then their bodies are larger than anticipated, jabbing their shoulders with fearsome beaks.

Your brother-in-law watches you sprint around the kitchen washing dishes for the holiday. Crusty pots, greasy pans, slick silverware and empty jars. You seize every item in sight and scrub. This is a polite way to avoid interaction. Nobody engages you, like hired help.

And as you navigate these domestic strains, there is a screen of untouched cold blind water, a layer of ice inside your heart, shut off from everyone. Your secrets are safe there.

Your nose runs and throat sore. You got the bartender's cold. None of this bothers you, his chills and coughs. You like being reminded of your human fragility. Forgiveness requires abrasions, symmetrical shadows. To take what you desire is to give your desire a name. And they say you're troubled, some people you know. They say you're troubled, but you've decided that trouble is just what they can't control. And they can't control you anymore. And if he is troubled, the bartender, it's the best trouble you've had in years.

At Rosh Hashana dinner, your brother-in-law speaks to you while you make sure everyone else is fed, and says, "There's a move in chess that made me think of you," he's referring to your interest in chess.

You played him once, this brother-in-law. He spent the entire game waxing on the strategies of chess, and you let him bloviate smug sardonic, until you silently beat him.

"There's a move in chess that made me think of you," he continues, "It's called the intercontinental ballistic missile. It's where you play and play, and you lose almost all your pieces. You lose so many pieces it looks like you're losing, but all you're doing is clearing the board. You're decluttering the center and making space for your queen to take my queen and put me in check."

And I knew then he had read me, my brother-in-law. The withdrawing of comforts, as Father once explained. To lose each piece, every figure and fortification, to make straight His paths.

II.

It's not the end. It can't be, you tell yourself, after they finish three biopsies for cancer. You cannot lift your eyes from the floor to the doctor as she repeats, "Today we got information, not answers."

"So, what kind of cancer is it?" the bartender asks as you both lie on your backs in the grass by the river. You don't answer and he continues, "Breast? Brain? Blood? Bone? If you could pick a cancer, what would it be?"

"Pancreatic," you reply, "the quickest and last to find."

In the middle of the night, you wake up, and he is gone. You call his name, but you don't know the dark halls of this house.

III.

X has noticed something detached in your gaze. You are wearing the clothes you slept in because you were out all-night with the bartender. You tell X you haven't eaten in two days. The first thing that passed your lips in forty-eight hours was a communion wafer. Off-hand, flippant, you mention that a jar of baby food is seventy-nine cents and seventy-five calories. Cheaper and more slimming than Ramen.

X tells you you're talking in non-sequiturs. He asks if you're alright and you ask what that means, to be alright. He follows you outside mid-morning. You tell him about the bartender.

X puts his arm around you and tells you you're a good person. You think his one-armed hug is a demonstration of good sportsmanship. A part of you put to sleep what you held onto for years with X. The totem of your youth. You've traversed some bridge. Of the friends you've lost, the homes you've relocated, the pounds you've shed, the money gone, it's only now the reprieve comes. You are too dazed to appreciate X's embrace at last. What you wanted for years. Your return to the office feels like trespassing into a previous home.

The following day X appears at work with a backpack filled with food and demands you eat it. He gives you an envelope with cash and asks you to take care of yourself. You can hardly look at him, just like the doctor, but he stays with you. Hours elapse but he sits patient beside you, speaking at length of secret things.

IV.

Your neighbor is sobbing and yelling. You can hear it in the hall as you come in from a cigarette. You knock on her door and offer to take her out.

"Breakfast, you don't even have to eat it," you tell her, "You can just take it home."

You go to a pricey market and get her a sandwich and groceries. She asks to make you a meal that night to return your kindness, but you tell her you have a date instead. The truth is you don't, but you hoped the bartender would call.

About the bartender, she asks, "Is he a man of God?"

You laugh and say, "No, but he's not hateful."

She pauses to take a bite of her sandwich and continues, "I think you need a man of God, someone who can pray alongside you."

The bartender does not call that night or the following night. You shower and cover yourself in perfumed creams in case he drops in like a crow from the branch.

V.

X texts you Sunday morning asking to see you. You walk to the park after church and see him on a bench, head lowered to book in hand. The noon church bells ring, their peals clanging about trees, booming over laughing children, dominating all present in the park. The mime is dancing for children, an old woman is asleep with her mouth open.

And you see X, you stand before him breathless in the sunlight. The bells plead around you like chaotic angels. He looks up at you, squinting in the sun, and you smile down at him, waiting.

The bells are roaring. They will not stand aside. In his wordless upward gaze from the bench, the wind picks up and you cling to your coat. You smile at each other, ablaze by midday glare.

VI.

One night, you are kneeling in church before the shrine of our Blessed Mother. You are rushing your words aloud, asking her to shield you and guide you, to bring you to her Son. That in your loneliness, despair, sin and strife, you pray to be available to God, to possess eyes that look outward to the needs of others. You pray for the Holy Spirit to move you in ways moving to the Holy Spirit. You thank the Lord for being more merciful to you than you were to yourself. You beg for the Virgin Mary's kindness and comfort, on your knees, eyes shut, candles flickering. You ask the Virgin Mary to be your mother when your own has not called you in weeks.

With eyes closed, still kneeling, you hear the church door clap shut. Someone descends the steps, shuffling past you. You keep praying aloud to our Lady. You don't care who hears you anymore, reciting a Hail Mary in Latin. A lowly broken creature petitioning God in the language of the angels. You ask the Lord for an increase of faith to dispel any shadow of disbelief. To have pity on your narrow vision, the confines of your passing appetites. You ask that God may help you hearken for things not of this world.

"In nomine patris et filii et spiritus sancti, amen." You sign the cross and gaze up at the statue of the Virgin Mary whose painted unblinking eyes stare ahead at the pews. Her nose is chipped. Your face is warmed by the yellow glow of votive candles.

You follow her gaze to the pews behind you, looking over your shoulder while kneeling. X is sitting in a pew with his back to you, listening to your prayers. You walk over and ask him to make room.

"I love you," he says.

Body.

Soul.

Composite.

Capitulum Octavum

I.

The world opened up as I knelt on the wood floor of my apartment between X's knees. The world opened up with his denim thighs astride my shoulders and my head on his chest, listening to his heartbeat. His hands found my shoulders, thumbs pressing slow circles in my back.

The world opened up as I clung to X, on my knees, on this same floor that only weeks before, after the biopsies, I lay upon with eyes registering the ceaseless whir of the ceiling fan. On my back on this floor with tears coating my face, surrendering my brief installment on earth.

The world opened up when for so long it felt closed. Not a penny to my name. When I would bump my cart with trash bags of clothes down a busy city sidewalk to the consignment shop, selling my belongings to buy groceries. When nobody would step aside for your cart with clothes on the sidewalk because they thought you were just some young homeless junkie.

The world opened up, when I felt like every friend was gone. When I cried in the dark clutching my rosary and could have sworn I felt the cells inside me darkening. That I could feel my insides seething with decay. Damaged goods.

The world opened up when I stood naked in front of the stove preparing a cherry cobbler and told X, "I don't want anyone to know about our lives." And he replied, "Our life."

II.

Because his lips are on you. Pressing out the words. Because his shirt evaporates as yours does. Because you're clinging to each other and knowing for the first time in a long time, the wordless ferocity of a bicep squeezing your rib cage, so tight in embrace the muscles tremble. A second virginity.

And then he holds you down by both wrists, moving against you, and you are a butterfly pinned, paper light and living for a second.

III.

"I need you to believe something," X says, holding both sides of your face, thumbs pressing the hollows of your cheeks, "You are so beautiful. I want you to believe this because I need you to survive."

You won't lift your eyes to his, you are embarrassed. He's referring to the trials you've subjected yourself to. Your invisibility test. The intense scrutiny of every morsel permitted inside you, after you permitted the wrong one. Damaged goods.

You are almost half the weight you were when you met him eight years ago. You shrunk two inches in height and one whole shoe size. Your features eroded by gale and gust so steadily, so imperceptibly, for so long, that to be seen again by another, anew, does not immediately penetrate. Scar tissue.

The corner of his mouth twitches with a smile and his eyes are wet. Years of torment, that weird little world you've constructed for yourself living alone, breaks open. Habits you thought not strange until an outsider approached, are discussed. One meal a day, a pickle spear and bottle of wine.

He delights in your cluttered apartment and says, "Everything in it is tiny like you."

And so secretly, and unbearably, you cover him with soft frantic kisses.

I believe the angels will save us. That as we lay in the dark, one stout orange candle burning, he asked me to marry him. While he sat on the edge of the bed, I knelt to the floor to tie his shoe, kissing the raised white band of a scar on his ankle. And somewhere long ago, he was thrown off that motorcycle and lived. I put away my pills and unpin my hair. Because I believe the angels will save us. They already have.

IV.

What if you got what you wanted most, after years of pining? Every friend gone, miring in debt, but just then, the secret wonder nursed behind your eye, emerges from a drawer you thought locked? How do you find your footing in the strange glow of his embrace, leaning on a light pole in front of your door, after you rushed your rosary breathless.

What do you do when it finally comes, your longings confessed aloud to the Lord on your knees in the last pew in the dark, materializes? When you've lost everything, including yourself, and the lone wish you dared not ask emerges like a moth from shadow. Like sudden spring rain driving down upon ice. How do you navigate this thaw?

You never asked the Lord to make X love you. This felt like a vain and shallow request, an unwelcome entreaty. That instead you should pray for those who are going without, those who are homebound bedridden and blind like your mother.

So instead, for years, you begged for the strength to bear rejection. To see all love as a loan. That perhaps if X did not love you, that Jesus too felt that scorn. A rejected stone becoming the cornerstone. That your knees wouldn't buckle under that cross. And we know not how we ought to pray and babble like pagans.

And what then, after X leaves you count the pills and estimate the hours of their effect, their half-life and where you'll be. If you'll be on a train, a sidewalk, or near a bathroom. X disrupted the arithmetic of your medicinal math. Your little habits are a lover you've taken in secret before X, this unmatched affair with your disintegration. You knead the soft layer of flesh around your naval with reproachful fingertips, a band of skin he nibbled gently hours earlier.

X reassures you, but you forged a friendship before him. A little private pact, the dark one that sidled up beside you when nobody else would, this demented dear friend. The ghost self. The shrinking self. The secret self you reclaimed, who handed you the indisputable authority to exact revenge. Obscene habits only grotesque when paired beside his affection.

X must be gone before sunrise. He must not open the bathroom cabinet. He chuckles at your small bathroom, its fuzzy floor mats and matching curtain.

One day you sit outside with X, and he smiles and tells you, "I saw you walking down the sidewalk, ahead of me, and you looked like a little doll. The way you move when you're going somewhere."

And you pause and tell him you have a disease, that you're a broken doll.

And as you close the bathroom door you pop the laxative by impulse. Checks and balances. You were so happy this week, you consumed tortillas and penne and peanut butter. You want to spare X from this monstrous thrall, the deranged hunger hiding inside. You know you could eat until your stomach hurts, until the skin atop your abdomen is sore from being stretched, bloated and tender, and still the hunger roars on.

The hunger is everywhere. You won't eat because you know how unstoppable you could be. Just like your mother, spooning ice cream over a crossword puzzle at the kitchen table midmorning. Who cannot feel her feet anymore. Picking through a taffy box.

I find myself inspecting the bodies of fat people with complete terror at inhabiting their frame. I see the ballooned gut with waistband straining against tucked shirt, ankles resembling fire hydrants, pendulous biceps, wobbling necks, fingers pinched by wedding bands. I have the soul of a fat person. My teeth cannot grind fast enough for my contracting gullet. I know I can radically eliminate every crust, crumb, and smear of sauce from a porcelain surface. I could eat myself to death like a dog.

The desires are unyielding. I burn it at the root by abstaining. A raging werewolf madness. You must keep the fur from coming through, the fangs from lengthening too prominent. You must trim yourself down. You longed for X so long you consigned yourself to loneliness. For it seems, when you have a knot you cannot unfasten, it is only when your fingers slacken, weary with waiting, that these mysteries unfold. You were a stray hound accustomed to unlit roads, eating rocks.

My heart is a thief. It steals over his flesh. Furtive glances flit across his thighs like phantom butterflies. My heart is a thief: faithless, ravenous, and alien unto myself. A beast of ignorant adoption. A servant of inconsistent training. An animal I could not domesticate. A roaming I could not mitigate. An infection I could not annihilate.

My heart is a thief given clemency by his unexpected love. I am finally being asked to quit this bloodletting. And now that you have permission to let go, you don't know where your hands are anymore. Hands that stole his breath as you placed him inside you. You can throw away the pills but not these hands.

My heart is a thief, it waits until nobody is looking to press the pills out of their aluminum bulbs. Pills pouched under the tongue like orange polyps, hastening out my insides, dipping down the scale. Loathe forbid the day out of hand, sneaking a Snickers in an alcove by a vending machine. Followed by penance. Cramps so intense they can be felt in the arches of your feet. That sleepwalk down the hall after, like you've been dazed by a mugging.

Your secret self-sculpture, your mission of self-erasure that accompanied you before X. This fatalistic sport, daring yourself to get thinner and thinner, arises from a place of no kisses. It's not a simple equation. It's a complex formula with conflicting variables, contingencies and calculations of meals divided by days, fasting multiplied by weeks. The Algorithms of Thin emerge from rejecting a null hypothesis of caloric proportion. A reservoir of feeling whose strength relies on its impossibility to be touched.

Despite these disordered affections, I choose X. My wrists locked into the mattress, pursued by his lowering hips.

I remind myself my life is a loan. All affections and afflictions a loan that can only be repaid by more deepened longing, a spreading stain darkening like storm clouds, welded to the sheets. We lay quiet on our backs, stunned. Our breath a loan. Our dewy leaden gazes register naught. One eye knows not of its other eye in the same skull, side by side affixed to the ceiling.

"I still don't know, if someone were to ask me, how I ended up here," he smirks while tying his shoe. Your wistful smile does not break in reply. Instead, you spread butter on bread, knife pressing into palm. The prayers you dared not speak were heard. You believe the Holy Spirit ferried him upon unknown tides, his sneakered feet scooped down the street by mysterious winds, into your studio apartment.

Once, a year before, you sat in church and gazed at the families during a homily. A child clanged a toy car against a radiator, and you held back tears, thinking you would never have that.

He bites into his honey sod toast with contented sigh. Your hand rests atop the table beside curly brown bacon, your hand found by his.

Dear Mr. Policeman, the search is over.

V.

It's an easy inspection. Alone in your office, you bunch your sleeve to your elbow and examine the bruise X gave you. Lovers' play. Wrestling atop your sheets and laughing the night before. Suddenly, the greenish polygon on your arm is a map of something animal and unseen. The outline of a hidden personality.

You did not anticipate his tenderness. The slow invisible string he pulls from the base of your spine to your shoulder blades. The overwhelming unspeakable nearness of his eyes, a stare you'd known so long only at arm's length, now deep in your bed, inches from your own. Your legs knit under sheets and the shade pulled down, your cheap coffee maker belching. A stilled hour that must confide, so secretly, that he is finally here.

And what of these strange little worlds we permit entry? You've taken ownership of a passport bound by the senses. An expatriate from a nether world of daytime obligations. You know not of hours evaporating, clothes scattered on the cold wood floor, messages unanswered.

To know then, the short cry released in his neck when he hugs you. And now he stands in your pocket-sized bedroom-kitchen, with his hands in his jacket, to confirm aloud in sleepy downward gaze, that you need to let yourself be loved. In his arms, you tell X:

"You're my one wish that came true."

VI.

Walking into the high school gymnasium, the smell of rubber and cleaning fluid smacks from the waxed floor. Dented gym mats tacked to the wall. Polyester pennants hang limp under high foggy windows. The bleachers are pulled out, taking up half the basketball court. The other side has a small stage with heavy red curtains drawn aside for a microphone.

At dawn, you hurried down the city sidewalk, buses roaring past, leaping over clumped vomit on the curb, scurrying into the train station. A fifty-minute ride later, you are on the campus of a small Catholic girls' school. You pass a jogger's trail called Poppy Jane Lane and an empty tennis court covered with leaves.

You have not been in a high school since your own a decade prior. Safety pinned earlobes, ripped plaid shoelaces in chunky heeled platform boots, dollar store matte red nail polish whose specks scattered across your overbite when you were nervous, nibbling a hang nail for a cigarette. You were called to this girls' school by a new teacher, a middle-aged divorcé you met at church months before while making sandwiches for the homeless. You were a PB & J machine, raspberry jam on your knuckles, hunkered down at a folding table in a musty rec hall. This schoolteacher sat across from you making ham and cheese for the homeless, and found your faith journey touching, the diligent Jew averse to small talk, becoming Catholic.

He reserved two senior classes for you this morning. Monday guest speaker. Three dozen girls shuffle into the gym to hear you speak. Rubbing their eyes and dragging back packs.

You are immersed in adolescent reveries and without word register: the girl with the faded band T shirt and large black framed glasses looking about peevishly for someone to sit beside her. Another girl that's late, arrives with a thermos and ignores the teacher's greeting. Another, tight bun and bright blue poncho, has a gaggle of girls fawning at her elaborate hand motions while instructing how to apply mascara. You were just about these girls' ages when you were in the mental hospitals. When you got the disease. When you thought you knew everything.

You are introduced and approach the podium. You apologize for looking down while reading your prepared notes, but the girls are unphased and half asleep. This is the first time you have told your story aloud to a group, a dazed platoon of female minors, yet unscathed by the world, small flowers whose freckled noses crinkle in curiosity.

As you are speaking you look up and pause over a sentence, you realize how many faces are staring back at you. Kids. The sincerity of their silence shocks you. For a moment you've lost your place in your typed paragraphs. Your voice hovers midair, only to notice one girl. On the end, far left. Wearing a fuzzy white sweater with a sequined American flag and her glassy black eyes stung with tears.

After you finish, the teacher asks the girls for questions. Some do, some have multiple. You address each with serene sisterly warmth. The girl in the sequined sweater, the one who watched you, her hand darts up just as the bell rings.

"Next period!" the teacher announces, and the girls gather their bags to file out. The girl in the sweater does not get up immediately but sits watching everyone push past her. She looks to the ground before pulling her backpack to her chest and rising slowly to her feet.

From the podium we both stare at each other. This girl and I. Her gaze aches with concern, like she wants to ask me something, but can't break away from the crowd.

I nod at her and smile. She will find her story someday like I did.

FINIS

www.ingramcontent.com/pod-product-compliance
Lightning Source LLC
Chambersburg PA
CBHW011118100726
47898CB00011B/3145

9780578732350